50 Muscle Building Shake Recipes for Weightlifting:

High Protein Content in Every Shake

By

Joseph Correa

Certified Sports Nutritionist

COPYRIGHT

© 2016 Finibi Inc

All rights reserved

Reproduction or translation of any part of this work beyond that permitted by section 107 or 108 of the 1976 United States Copyright Act without the permission of the copyright owner is unlawful.

This publication is designed to provide accurate and authoritative information in regard to the subject matter covered. It is sold with the understanding that neither the author nor the publisher is engaged in rendering medical advice. If medical advice or assistance is needed, consult with a doctor. This book is considered a guide and should not be used in any way detrimental to your health. Consult with a physician before starting this nutritional plan to make sure it's right for you.

ACKNOWLEDGEMENTS

The realization and success of this book could not have been possible without the motivation and support of my entire family.

50 Muscle Building Shake Recipes for Weightlifting:

High Protein Content in Every Shake

By

Joseph Correa

Certified Sports Nutritionist

CONTENTS

Copyright

Acknowledgements

About The Author

Introduction

Calendar

50 Muscle Building Shake Recipes for Weightlifting: High Protein Content in Every Shake

Other Great Titles by This Author

ABOUT THE AUTHOR

As a certified sports nutritionist, I honestly believe in the positive effects that proper nutrition can have over the body and mind. My knowledge and experience has helped me live healthier throughout the years and which I have shared with family and friends. The more you know about eating and drinking healthier, the sooner you will want to change your life and eating habits.

Nutrition is a key part in the process of being healthy and living longer so get started today.

INTRODUCTION

50 Muscle Building Shake Recipes for Weightlifting will help you increase the amount of protein you consume per day to help increase muscle mass. These shakes will help increase muscle in an organized manner by adding large and healthy portions of protein to your diet. Being too busy to eat right can sometimes become a problem and that's why this book will save you time and help nourish your body to achieve the goals you want. Make sure you know what you're consuming by preparing it yourself or having someone prepare it for you.

This book will help you to:

-Gain muscle fast.

-Save time.

-Have more energy.

-Train harder and longer.

-Naturally accelerate Your Metabolism to build more muscle.

-Improve your digestive system.

Joseph Correa is a certified sports nutritionist and a professional athlete.

50 MUSCLE BUILDING SHAKE RECIPES

Day 1

Breakfast: All in one shake

Energy, Muscle Gain Shake

Preparation:

Mix all the ingredients together in a juicer or blender at high speed and then enjoy a delicious shake.

We all know how hard it is to gain muscle; we always need some help with this problem. So here is a great shake to improve muscle gain and also strengthen the body. You can drink it any time of the day, but we suggest breakfast as a good time.

Ingredients:

- Milk, 400 ml
- 2 scoops Whey Protein Powder
- 2 banana 140g
- Almond oil 2 tbsp.
- 1 apple

Nutrition facts:

- Calories: 443
- Proteins: 32.5 g
- Carbs: 45 g
- Fat: 16 g

Day 2

Lunch: Get big Shake

Muscle Gain Shake

Preparation:

Mix all the ingredients together in a juicer or blender at high speed and then enjoy a delicious shake.

Eat big to get big that is the secret to building large amounts of muscle mass based mainly on a high percentage of protein's. To reach that goal you have to put a lot of effort and eat right, here is a great shake to help you with this.

Ingredients:

- ½ cup unsweetened almond milk
- 2 tbsp. maple syrup
- 2 frozen bananas
- 1 scoop whey protein powder
- 3 tbsp. of almond butter

Nutritional facts:

- Calories – 830

- Total fat- 30g (healthy fat from almond butter)
- Carbs – 115g
- Fiber- 14g
- Net Carbs -101 g
- Gluten Free
- Protein: 46 g

Day 3

Breakfast: No powder Shake

Muscle gain shake

Preparation:

Mix all the ingredients together in a juicer or blender at high speed and then enjoy a delicious shake.

Get the most out of your mix with this great recipe. Running out of time, and yet you want to achieve your nutritional quota, this delicious drink is ready in less than a minute. Your body needs a protein rich milkshake "super" for your muscles that will give you a good balance of carbohydrates and protein and what better way to do this than with this mix of ingredients.

Ingredients:

- Almond oil 2 tbsp.
- 2 tbsp. Peanut Butter
- ½ - 1 tsp Honey
- 1 medium Banana
- 2 cups Milk
- 2 scoops Whey Protein powder

Nutrition Facts:

- Calories: 601
- Protein: 49 g
- Carbs: 63 g
- Fat: 25 g

Day 4

Breakfast: Coffee Protein Shake

Muscle Gain Shake

Preparation:

Mix all the ingredients together in a juicer or blender at high speed and then enjoy a delicious shake.

This shake recipe takes seconds to make, and will be a tasty one. Make sure you use all the ingredients, blend them well and serve it after a training session. Muscle gain is one of the hardest things to achieve at the gym, so any help you can get will definitely be worth the effort.

Ingredients:

- 2 scoops Whey Protein powder
- 8 ounces Coffee
- 8 ounces 2% Milk
- 2 tbsp. Caramel Creamer

Nutrition facts:

- Calories: 398

- Protein 58.4 g
- Carbs 13.4 g
- Fat 6.4 g

Day 5

Breakfast: Peanut Butter Bulking Protein Shake

Muscle Gain Shake

Preparation:

Mix all the ingredients together in a juicer or blender at high speed and then enjoy a delicious shake.

This shake recipe is a great one to improve your performance in the gym and to increase muscle growth. Place ingredients into a blender until smooth. You might also want to use whole milk and additional peanut butter to turn this protein shake into a higher calorie weight gainer, it's up to you.

Ingredients:

- 8 oz. skim milk
- 1 banana
- 1 tbsp. peanut butter
- 2 scoops of whey protein powder

Nutritional facts:

- Calories 498
- Protein 58 g
- Carbs 44.1 g
- Fat 11 g

Day 6

Breakfast: Pink Super Shake

Muscle Gain Shake

Preparation:

Mix all the ingredients together in a juicer or blender at high speed and then enjoy a delicious shake.

When it comes to massive weight increases, it's more important to consume the right amount of calories from a proper ratio of carbohydrates to protein so you have enough energy to train and enough protein to allow your muscles to develop.

Ingredients:

- ¾ cup organic frozen raspberries
- ½ small banana
- 1 scoop whey protein powder
- ½ tbsp. raw coconut butter
- 5 g glutamine
- 1 cup spring water

Nutritional facts:

- Calories: 268
- Protein : 16.5 g
- Carbs: 44.5 g
- Fat 6.7 g

Day 7

Breakfast: Banana Protein Shake

Muscle Gain Shake

Proteins are the most important nutrients for muscle growth. They ensure that the body functions properly. For practitioners of bodybuilding, they allow you to have bigger muscles provided, of course, you follow appropriate training, and you have a healthy diet. This is an easy-to-prepare shake that has a large amount of protein.

Preparation:

Mix all the ingredients together in a juicer or blender at high speed and then enjoy a delicious shake.

Ingredients:

- 8 oz. skim milk
- 1 banana
- ½ cups of oats
- 2 scoops of whey protein powder

Nutritional facts:

- Calories 554
- Protein 58g
- Carbs 67.5g
- Fat 6g

Day 8

Breakfast: Banana Berry Protein Shake

Gaining Mass Protein shake

This is a great shake for gaining strength and mass in a short period of time, with no delays. It's healthy, natural, and will make a big impact in your gym routine. So let's see the ingredients and all that it has to offer you.

Preparation:

Mix all the ingredients together in a juicer or blender at high speed and then enjoy a delicious shake.

Ingredients:

- 12 ounces of water
- 4 ice cubes
- 1 banana
- 2 scoops of whey protein

Nutritional facts:

- Calories 314
- Protein 45.1g

- Carbs: 32.1g
- Fat 2.4g

Day 9

Breakfast: Almond and Banana Thirst

Gaining Mass Shake

Increase your muscle gain using this shake recipe, and then track your progress the day after you've trained to see if it helped your performance. You could even prepare it the night before in order to make all the ingredients combine even better.

Preparation:

Mix all the ingredients together in a juicer or blender at high speed and then enjoy a delicious shake.

Ingredients:

- 1 frozen medium banana
- 1 cup plain yogurt
- 100 ml ice cold water
- 1 ounce ground almonds
- 1 cup raw oats

Nutritional facts:

- Calories: 650

- Protein: 53 g
- Carbs: 75 g
- Fat: 15 g

Day 10

Lunch: Cinnamon Protein Shake

Gaining Muscle Shake

Follow this shake recipe to increase your muscle gain, with a low fat intake. You can drink this shake any time of the day.

Preparation:

Mix all the ingredients together in a juicer or blender at high speed and then enjoy a delicious shake.

Ingredients:

- 1 cup Skim Milk
- 1 frozen Banana
- 1 scoop Whey Protein Powder
- 1 tbsp. Peanut Butter

Nutritional Facts:

- Calories: 391
- Protein: 38g
- Carbs: 42.1g
- Fat: 10g

Day 11

Breakfast: Heavy gainer Shake

Gaining Mass Shake

Here is a great shake recipe that will give you a huge boost of energy and also will help increasing your muscle development. So be ready for a great experience that will improve your gym sessions.

Preparation:

Mix all the ingredients together in a juicer or blender at high speed and then enjoy a delicious shake.

Ingredients:

- 10-14 oz. pure water
- 1/2 cup raw almonds
- 1/2 large frozen banana
- 2 scoops whey protein powder

Nutritional facts:

- Calories: 380
- Proteins: 75 g

- Carbs: 57 g
- Fat: 15 g

Day 12

Breakfast: Extreme Energy Shake

Gaining mass and energy Shake

If you were looking for something to supply you with some extra energy and also improve your muscle growth you should go for this shake recipe. This shake is full of healthy ingredients. Green Tea has been said to prevent cancer and flax seeds provide a good serving of omega 3 which is important for your body's development.

Preparation:

Mix all the ingredients together in a juicer or blender at high speed and then enjoy a delicious shake.

Ingredients:

- 10 oz. pure water
- 10 strawberries (Fresh or Frozen)
- 1 tbs. flax-seed oil
- 1/2 tsp Green Tea Powder
- 1/2 tsp vanilla extract
- 1 scoop Whey Protein Powder

Nutritional Facts:

- Calories: 420
- Protein: 50 g
- Carbs: 42 g
- Fat: 17 g

Day 13

Lunch: Peaches Shake

Gaining muscle Shake

The peaches in this shake give it a great flavor and cottage cheese is an excellent source of protein and is easy to digest. The best time of the day to drink this shake would be in the morning but you can drink it any time.

Preparation:

Mix all the ingredients together in a juicer or blender at high speed and then enjoy a delicious shake.

Ingredients:

- 8 oz. pure water
- 1 ripe peach
- 2 tbs. low-fat cottage cheese
- Brown sugar
- 1.5 scoop whey protein powder

Nutritional Facts:

- Calories: 250

- Proteins: 40 g
- Carbs: 21 g
- Fat: 8 g

Day 14

Breakfast: Blueberry Shake

Gaining muscle Shake

Let's start the day off with a great shake recipe that will maintain your energy levels high, and provide the required protein intake so you can increase more muscle in a shorter time period. Blueberries are known to be great antioxidants and help prevent cancer.

Preparation:

Mix all the ingredients together in a juicer or blender at high speed and then enjoy a delicious shake.

Ingredients:

- 10 oz. Pure water
- 1/2 cup fresh or frozen blueberries
- 1.5 scoop whey protein powder
- 2 tsp. flax-seed oil

Nutritional Facts:

- Calories: 210 g
- Proteins: 39g

- Carbs: 22 g
- Fat: 4 g

Day 15

Breakfast: Strawberry Shake

Gaining muscle Shake

There is no better way of getting fast results when trying to get muscle growth, than using shakes and this shake recipe will taste delicious because of the combination of strawberries and cottage cheese.

Preparation:

Mix all the ingredients together in a juicer or blender at high speed and then enjoy a delicious shake.

Ingredients:

- 10 oz. pure water
- 8 frozen strawberries
- 4 tbs. low-fat cottage cheese
- 1.5 scoop whey protein powder

Nutritional Facts:

- Calories: 310 g
- Proteins: 51g

- Carbs: 27g
- Fat: 7 g

Day 16

Breakfast: Banana delight Shake

Gaining muscle Shake

Combine the following ingredients to get a shake high in omega 3 and high in potassium to help you increase muscle gain, and also maintain a healthy body.

Preparation:

Mix all the ingredients together in a juicer or blender at high speed and then enjoy a delicious shake.

Ingredients:

- 8 oz. pure water
- 1/2 banana (frozen)
- 2 scoops whey protein powder
- 2 tsp. flax-seed oil

Nutritional Facts:

- Calories: 350 g
- Proteins: 65g

- Carbs: 29g
- Fat: 9 g

Day 17

Breakfast: Pineapple Shake

Gaining muscle Shake

Try this amazing shake recipe that is well known for fast results and delicious taste. It's perfect to help you increase your muscle gain, and will have a strong effect on your immune system.

Preparation:

Mix all the ingredients together in a juicer or blender at high speed and then enjoy a delicious shake.

Ingredients:

- 1 cup of pineapple juice
- 3 strawberries
- 1 banana
- 1 tsp. of yogurt
- 1 scoop whey protein powder

Nutritional Facts:

- Calories: 340 g

- Proteins: 63g
- Carbs: 27g
- Fat: 10 g

Day 18

Breakfast: Muscle Shake

Gaining muscle Shake

Having problems getting bigger muscles? If the answer is yes, you should try this shake recipe that will bring instant results in your training and energy throughout the day.

Preparation:

Mix all the ingredients together in a juicer or blender at high speed and then enjoy a delicious shake.

Ingredients:

- 1 c. low-fat milk
- 1/2 c. plain low-fat yogurt
- 1 banana, sliced
- 2 tbsp. Whey Protein Powder
- 6 strawberries, sliced
- 1 tsp. wheat germ
- 1 tbsp. honey or maple syrup
- 1/4 cup of any frozen berries

- Pinch of nutmeg or carob powder

Nutritional Facts:

- Calories: 600
- Proteins: 70g
- Carbs: 54g
- Fat: 15 g

Day 19

Breakfast: Oatmeal Shake

Gaining muscle Shake

This is a great shake recipe to increase muscle mass and protect your heart. It will help you stay alert during the entire day, go for it.

Preparation:

Mix all the ingredients together in a juicer or blender at high speed and then enjoy a delicious shake.

Ingredients:

- 2 scoops whey protein powder
- 1 cup sugar-free vanilla ice cream
- 1 cup oatmeal
- 2 cups non-fat milk
- 1.2 cup water
- A splash of peppermint extract!

Nutritional Facts:

- Calories: 621

- Proteins: 65g
- Carbs: 58g
- Fat: 22 g

Day 20

Lunch: Tropical Shake

Gaining muscle Shake

This is one of the most delicious shakes I have ever tasted and I am sure you will enjoy it. The mix between banana, pineapple, and coconut gives it a tropical flavor that should go well in the morning or mid-morning. The bananas don't have to be frozen, they can be room temperature but some people prefer that it be cold if they have just finished working out.

Preparation:

Mix all the ingredients together in a juicer or blender at high speed and then enjoy a delicious shake.

Ingredients:

- 8 oz. pure water
- 1/2 tsp. pineapple extract
- 1/2 tsp. coconut extract
- 1 tbsp. cottage cheese
- 1/2 frozen banana

Nutritional Facts:

- Calories: 540
- Proteins: 25g
- Carbs: 43g
- Fat: 17g

Day 21

Lunch: Fruit Shake

Gaining muscle Shake

Protein is the key to muscle growth and recovery. Make sure you try this shake at any time of the day. This berry shake has many antioxidant qualities that will benefit you as you age and will prevent you from getting sick as often and that can be very important when you can't afford to take week long breaks from working out.

Preparation:

Mix all the ingredients together in a juicer or blender at high speed and then enjoy a delicious shake.

Ingredients:

- 2 scoops Milk protein powder
- 4 large strawberries
- blueberries (a small handful)
- water (just a few drops)
- 3 eggs

Nutritional Facts:

- Calories: 470
- Proteins: 45g
- Carbs: 39g
- Fat: 15g

Day 22

Breakfast: Apple Pie Delight Shake

Muscle gain Shake

Athletes who consume more protein will increase more muscle mass than sedentary people because they maximize growth potential so try to make sure you add this shake just before or just after a training session. The mixture of flavors from apple, cinnamon, and nutmeg give an original flavor not normally found in other shakes.

Preparation:

Mix all the ingredients together in a juicer or blender at high speed and then enjoy a delicious shake.

Ingredients:

- 1 scoop Whey protein powder
- 1 peeled and cored apple, cut into pieces
- 1 1/2 cups of milk
- 1/2 tsp cinnamon
- 1/2 tsp nutmeg
- 5 Ice Cubes

Nutritional Facts:

- Calories: 350
- Proteins: 35g
- Carbs: 21g
- Fat: 10g

Day 23

Breakfast: Pumpkin Shake

Low on carbs Shake

Here's one shake for you that's a great source of protein and provides a high level of energy during the day. The flax oil and yogurt provide you with several ingredients for your bodies overall function and help give this shake a boost of calcium and omega 3.

Preparation:

Mix all the ingredients together in a juicer or blender at high speed and then enjoy a delicious shake.

Ingredients:

- 2 Scoops Milk protein powder
- 8 oz. water
- 1 tbsp. Flax oil
- 1 tsp. Pumpkin pie spice
- 8 oz. Yogurt
- 4-6 ice cubes

Nutritional Facts:

- Calories: 300
- Proteins: 40g
- Carbs: 26g
- Fat: 11g

Day 24

Breakfast: Cinnamon Shake

Muscle gain Shake

This shake should be consumed early in the morning before a training session because it's a good energy provider and will also help accelerate muscle recovery.

Preparation:

Mix all the ingredients together in a juicer or blender at high speed and then enjoy a delicious shake.

Ingredients:

- 1 graham cracker
- 1/2 tsp cinnamon
- vanilla extract
- 12oz. water
- 4 Ice Cubes

Nutritional Facts:

- Calories: 280

- Proteins: 10g
- Carbs: 15g
- Fat: 5g

Day 25

Breakfast: Peanut Butter and Banana Shake

Muscle gain Shake

Peanut butter is a great source of protein and energy. Many athletes use peanut butter as a main source of energy before training or before competing. The banana and almond content improve the flavor and make it even more digestive.

Preparation:

Mix all the ingredients together in a juicer or blender at high speed and then enjoy a delicious shake.

Ingredients:

- 2 scoops Whey Protein Powder
- 100g almond slices
- 1 tbsp. peanut butter
- 500ml skim milk
- half banana
- 1 table-spoon honey

Nutritional Facts:

- Calories: 600
- Proteins: 55g
- Carbs: 35g
- Fat: 10g

Day 26

Breakfast: Super Mix Shake

Muscle gain Shake

Depending on your metabolism, you will adapt to some of the shakes better than others. For those of you who prefer a sweeter flavor in your shakes, this is a good choice. You can adapt certain ingredients to change the flavor to your preference like the caramel, hazelnuts, or vanilla yogurt.

Preparation:

Mix all the ingredients together in a juicer or blender at high speed and then enjoy a delicious shake.

Ingredients:

- 10 Ice Cubes
- 12 oz. fat-free milk
- 2 tbsp. fat free vanilla yogurt or Kefir
- 1 tbsp. reduced fat peanut butter
- 2 tbsp. spoon hazelnuts
- 1 tbsp. caramel ice cream topping

Nutritional Facts:

- Calories: 430
- Proteins: 23g
- Carbs: 20g
- Fat: 11g

Day 27

Breakfast: Lean mass Banana Shake

Muscle gain Shake

People who stick to a muscle gain diet or routine will benefit even more if they add muscle shakes because of the ease of preparation and because of how fast the body can absorb the protein and nutrients.

Preparation:

Mix all the ingredients together in a juicer or blender at high speed and then enjoy a delicious shake.

Ingredients:

- 1/2 frozen banana
- 2 tbsp. Whipping cream (heavy cream, not cream out of a can)
- 2 eggs
- 10-12 oz. water
- 4-6 ice cubes

Nutritional Facts:

- Calories: 320
- Proteins: 18g
- Carbs: 15g
- Fat: 9g

Day 28

Lunch: Sweet Boost Shake

Muscle gain Shake

Here is a great example of a shake recipe that has very different ingredients, but combined they are a great source of protein and will increase your gym performance.

Preparation:

Mix all the ingredients together in a juicer or blender at high speed and then enjoy a delicious shake.

Ingredients:

- 1 medium to large banana
- 8 oz. light Milk
- 1 tbsp. Flaxseed and Almond Mixture
- 1 tsp Maple Syrup
- Few drops of vanilla essence/extract
- 3-4 cubes ice
- 1 tbsp. low-fat natural yogurt

Nutritional Facts:

- Calories: 450
- Proteins: 19g
- Carbs: 16g
- Fat: 10g

Day 29

Breakfast: Orange Shake

Muscle gain Shake

Let's start the day with an awesome shake to boost our immune system and help you increase more muscle. This recipe is high in vitamin C and potassium because of the strawberries and orange juice which will also allow your muscles to recover faster.

Preparation:

Mix all the ingredients together in a juicer or blender at high speed and then enjoy a delicious shake.

Ingredients:

- 8 oz. Orange Juice
- 4-5 ice cubes
- 1 tsp. Vanilla Extract
- ½ banana
- 2-3 frozen strawberries
- 2 tsp. honey

Nutritional Facts:

- Calories: 291
- Proteins: 15g
- Carbs: 12g
- Fat: 5g

Day 30

Breakfast: Almond Shake Blast

Muscle gain Shake

Plan on having a better digestion after having this shake with this combination of oatmeal, raisins, almonds, and peanut butter. The raisins give it a great flavor and the oatmeal gives it a different texture than other shakes.

Preparation:

Mix all the ingredients together in a juicer or blender at high speed and then enjoy a delicious shake.

Ingredients:

- 10-12 oz. of skim milk
- 1.2 cup of raw oatmeal
- 1.2 cup of raisins
- 12 shredded almonds
- 1 tbsp. of peanut butter.

Nutritional Facts:

- Calories: 380

- Proteins: 18g
- Carbs: 15g
- Fat: 12g

Day 31

Breakfast: Wild berry Shake

Muscle Gain Shake

Raspberries are known to be very high on vitamin C and antioxidants which many medical professionals suggest as an anti-cancer supplement to your normal day to day foods and meals. It's the perfect mixture for those who want to gain muscle mass and strength. You can replace an ordinary snack with this healthy drink that is not very high on protein but will help take a break from all the other high protein shakes you will be taking on a daily basis.

Preparation:

Mix all the ingredients together in a juicer or blender at high speed and then enjoy a delicious shake.

Ingredients:

- 8 raspberries
- 4 strawberries
- 15 blueberries
- 16 ounces non-fat milk
- 1/2 cup ice cubes

Nutritional Facts:

- Calories: 210
- Proteins: 9g
- Carbs: 10g
- Fat: 8g

Day 32

Breakfast: Peanut Banana Shake

Muscle Gain Shake

In terms of nutrition this shake is high on lean protein and complex carbs, so it will increase muscle growth and recovery. It will also give you an energy boost while your training if you drink it half hour before.

Preparation:

Mix all the ingredients together in a juicer or blender at high speed and then enjoy a delicious shake.

Ingredients:

- ½ cup Peanuts
- 1/2 Banana
- 1 Cup Skim Milk
- 1/4 Cup Quaker Oats
- 2 Ice Cubes
- Pinch of Salt

Nutritional Facts:

- Calories: 230
- Proteins: 18g
- Carbs: 12g
- Fat: 5g

Day 33

Breakfast: Carrot Pineapple Shake

Muscle Gain Shake

This shake might look a little strange for you guys, but believe me it's a good one for you and your body. You can remove or lower the portions for some of the ingredients depending on your preference as this mix is very different from some of the others.

Preparation:

Mix all the ingredients together in a juicer or blender at high speed and then enjoy a delicious shake.

Ingredients:

- 1 cup chocolate milk
- 3/4 c shredded carrots
- 10 frozen pineapple chunks
- 2 tsp unsweetened shredded coconut
- 1 tsp vanilla
- 1 tsp sweet cream

- 4 oz. Neufchatel Cheese or cream cheese

Nutritional Facts:

- Calories: 220
- Proteins: 21g
- Carbs: 13g
- Fat: 13g

Day 34

Lunch: Pumpkin Shake

Muscle Gain Shake

Great shake recipe to help you increase your muscle gain and strength with a very unique taste that makes it fun to drink while still consuming a decent amount of protein. It's the perfect supplement for muscle recovery and muscle gain.

Preparation:

Mix all the ingredients together in a juicer or blender at high speed and then enjoy a delicious shake.

Ingredients:

- 3/4 c. milk (whatever kind you like)
- 1/4 c. canned pumpkin
- 1 tbsp. Pumpkin Pie flavored syrup
- 1/2 tsp. pumpkin pie spice
- 10 ice cubes

Nutritional Facts:

- Calories: 235

- Proteins: 20g
- Carbs: 17g
- Fat: 1.5g

Day 35

Breakfast: Blueberry Apple Shake

Energy Boost Shake

Maintaining a high level of energy is the goal of this shake. It will also provide you with some lean proteins that will help you even if you're a bit tired that day or if you just want to push yourself harder that day.

Preparation:

Mix all the ingredients together in a juicer or blender at high speed and then enjoy a delicious shake.

Ingredients:

- 1/2 small apple cut into small pieces (with skin)
- 1/2 cup cherries (dark, sweet, pitted)
- 1/2 cup blueberries
- 4 tbsp. wheat germ
- ice cubes (if desired)
- 1/2 cup whey protein

Nutritional Facts:

- Calories:300
- Proteins: 39g
- Carbs: 18g
- Fat: 5g

Day 36

Breakfast: Cherry Banana

Energy Boost Shake

Two great tasting ingredients in one shake. Cherries and bananas are provide a great source of fiber that your body needs when taking in large portions of protein. Try this drink before any training session night or day.

Preparation:

Mix all the ingredients together in a juicer or blender at high speed and then enjoy a delicious shake.

Ingredients:

- 1/2 cup cherries (dark, sweet, pitted)
- 1/2 cup Banana
- 4 tbsp. wheat germ
- ice cubes (if desired)
- 1/2 cup whey protein

Nutritional Facts:

- Calories:300

- Proteins: 39g
- Carbs: 18g
- Fat: 5g

Day 37

Breakfast: Egg Mania Shake

Muscle Gain Shake

You can have a muscle gain shake recipe with no protein powder in it and still intake a good amount of protein. The chick peas give it a green color but don't really change the flavor at all. This is a great combination of proteins and carbs.

Preparation:

Mix all the ingredients together in a juicer or blender at high speed and then enjoy a delicious shake.

Ingredients:

- 4 egg whites
- 1/2 cup cottage cheese
- 1 banana
- 1/4 cup chick peas
- pineapple slices
- Coconut milk
- Coconut extract can be added

- ice cubes

Nutritional Facts:

- Calories: 280
- Proteins: 25g
- Carbs: 40g
- Fat: 4g

Day 38

Breakfast: High Protein Shake

Muscle Gain Shake

Increase your gym performance by increase the amounts of protein you have on a daily basis. This shake is high on protein and high on flavor.

Preparation:

Mix all the ingredients together in a juicer or blender at high speed and then enjoy a delicious shake.

Ingredients:

- 1/2 c water
- 1 scoop Whey Protein Powder
- 2 tbsp. Honey
- 1 tbsp. Smooth Peanut Butter
- 1/2 cup Ice

Nutritional Facts:

- Calories:114

- Proteins: 34g
- Carbs: 5.2g
- Fat: 4.5g

Day 39

Breakfast: Fruit Mix Shake

Muscle Gain Shake

This shake recipe can easily replace your breakfast but this still have a healthy portion of food to nourish your body. It has a lot of the nutrients your body needs to have a good start in the morning. Protein and carbs are included in this recipe to give your energy and strength when training.

Preparation:

Mix all the ingredients together in a juicer or blender at high speed and then enjoy a delicious shake.

Ingredients:

- 1/2 banana chopped
- 1/2 cup of chopped strawberries
- 1 small apple
- 1 small plum
- 1 cup of chocolate milk
- 1 tbsp. of smooth peanut butter
- 1 scoop Whey Protein Powder

Nutritional Facts:

- Calories: 700
- Proteins: 46g
- Carbs: 90g
- Fat: 20g

Day 40

Breakfast: Choco Shake

Muscle Gain Shake

A great way of combining a dark chocolate bar with the right ingredients to obtain a shake that will increase your gym performance and muscle gain.

Preparation:

Mix all the ingredients together in a juicer or blender at high speed and then enjoy a delicious shake.

Ingredients:

- 1 dark chocolate bar
- 4 eggs
- 3 cups milk
- 1 scoop Whey Protein Powder

Nutritional Facts:

- Calories: 290
- Proteins: 45g

- Carbs: 37g
- Fat: 19g

Day 41

Breakfast: Taste of Everything Shake

Muscle Gain Shake

This shake recipe is an excellent source of protein and fiber your body needs. It's full of nutrients and vitamins that will you both bigger muscles and more energy when training to build more muscles.

Preparation:

Mix all the ingredients together in a juicer or blender at high speed and then enjoy a delicious shake.

Ingredients:

- Grapes, 4 grapes, seedless
- Blackberries, fresh, 0.5 grams
- Blueberries, fresh, 25 berries
- Strawberries, fresh, 0.5 grams
- Pineapple, fresh, 1 slice, thin (3-1/2" diameter x 1/2" thick
- Apples, fresh, 10 grams
- Yogurt, plain, low fat, 0.5 container (4 oz.)

- Kale, 0.5 grams
- Broccoli, fresh, 1 stalk
- Oranges, 0.5 grams
- 1 scoop Whey Protein Powder

Nutritional Facts:

- Calories: 280
- Proteins: 48g
- Carbs: 31g
- Fat: 4.2g

Day 42

Breakfast: Wake up Now Shake

Muscle Gain Shake

Here is how you should start the day, energy will be the defining word for this shake, but don't think it's not good for gaining muscle too, because you would be wrong.

Preparation:

Mix all the ingredients together in a juicer or blender at high speed and then enjoy a delicious shake.

Ingredients:

- 1 fresh banana, medium
- 2 servings (60 grs) oat flakes
- 1-2 tbsp. peanut butter, smooth style
- 1 cup (250 ml) yogurt, plain, low fat (0% - 1.5% mf)
- 0.5 tbsp. (or less) cinnamon, ground

Nutritional Facts:

- Calories:650

- Proteins: 28g
- Carbs: 85g
- Fat: 10g

Day 43

Lunch: Mango Tango Shake

Muscle Gain Shake

This is a great shake you can add to other days so you can take two shakes per day since it is high on fiber and low on fat. This lean shake will help you fight any tiredness in the gym and will improve your performance.

Preparation:

Mix all the ingredients together in a juicer or blender at high speed and then enjoy a delicious shake.

Ingredients:

- 2 large strawberries, fresh or frozen
- 10 blueberries, fresh or frozen
- 1 cup Orange Juice
- 1/2 mango, fresh or frozen
- 1 scoop Milk Protein Powder

Nutritional Facts:

- Calories:250

- Proteins: 30.5g
- Carbs: 52g
- Fat: 8.4g

Day 44

Breakfast: Pineapple Tangerine Shake

Muscle Gain Shake

To gain muscle, there is no secret; you have to train and eat right! You will struggle if you don't have enough energy while training and that's why adding ingredients that will give you a boost when necessary will make all the difference when trying to build stronger muscles.

Preparation:

Mix all the ingredients together in a juicer or blender at high speed and then enjoy a delicious shake.

Ingredients:

- 1/2 cup Pineapple, frozen chunks
- 1/2 cup Tangerines, (mandarin oranges), canned
- 2 tsp. honey
- 1 scoop Whey Protein Powder

Nutritional Facts:

- Calories:150

- Proteins: 39g
- Carbs: 17g
- Fat: 11g

Day 45

Breakfast: Peanut Butter Apple Shake

Muscle Gain Shake

Shakes can be a great source of calories and energy which are necessary to increase muscle mass. This delicious shake recipe is made to help you increase your muscle gain and maintain a high level of energy.

Preparation:

Mix all the ingredients together in a juicer or blender at high speed and then enjoy a delicious shake.

Ingredients:

- 3/4 Cup plain or vanilla yogurt
- 2 tbsp. Peanut Butter
- 1 Banana
- 1/8 Cup milk
- 3/4 Cup ice
- 1 apple

Nutritional Facts:

- Calories: 440
- Proteins: 22g
- Carbs: 50g
- Fat: 19g

Day 46

Breakfast: Banana Super Shake

Muscle Gain Shake

Vanilla almond milk will make this a great protein shake. It promotes muscle mass growth without unbalancing your diet. You can reduce or eliminate the cinnamon to make it to your specific preference.

Preparation:

Mix all the ingredients together in a juicer or blender at high speed and then enjoy a delicious shake.

Ingredients:

- 1/2 cup vanilla almond milk
- 1/2 cup water
- 1/2 banana
- Dash of cinnamon
- 1 scoop of vanilla protein powder

Nutritional Facts:

- Calories:350

- Proteins: 43g
- Carbs: 25g
- Fat: 5g

Day 47

Breakfast: Dark Oat Power Shake

Muscle Gain Shake

The combination of dark chocolate, cottage cheese, and oatmeal will increase your muscle development, and get you that energy boost that you were looking for in the gym while improve digestion and strengthening your heart.

Preparation:

Mix all the ingredients together in a juicer or blender at high speed and then enjoy a delicious shake.

Ingredients:

- 1/2 cup of Cottage Cheese (or 1 cup Greek yoghurt)
- 1/2 - 1 cup water (depending on desired thickness) or milk
- 10g dark chocolate
- ½ cup raw oatmeal
- 1/2 banana
- 1 scoop Whey Protein Powder

Nutritional Facts:

- Calories: 150
- Proteins: 40g
- Carbs: 20g
- Fat: 8g

Day 48

Breakfast: Milk Protein Shake

Muscle Gain Shake

To build and maintain your muscle mass you need to increase carbohydrates and protein so that you have the energy to work hard and the ingredients to allow your muscles to fully develop.

Preparation:

Mix all the ingredients together in a juicer or blender at high speed and then enjoy a delicious shake.

Ingredients:

- 1 scoop Milk protein powder
- 1/2 bananas
- 1/2 cup almond slices
- 8 oz milk
- 3 ice cubes

Nutritional Facts:

- Calories:335

- Proteins: 31g
- Carbs: 25g
- Fat: 18g

Day 49

Breakfast: Avocado Shake

Muscle Gain Shake

Protein shakes with vegetables are uncommon but should be more normal because of the value they bring to your diet and to your body. Avocado is considered by some as a "super food" and is great for your body.

Preparation:

Mix all the ingredients together in a juicer or blender at high speed and then enjoy a delicious shake.

Ingredients:

- 1/2 avocado
- 1 tbsp. shredded coconut
- 1 cup almond milk
- 1 scoop Whey Protein Powder

Nutritional Facts:

- Calories:300
- Proteins: 35g

- Carbs: 20g
- Fat: 8g

Day 50

Breakfast: Very Berry Shake

Muscle Gain Shake

A complete berry and protein combination to improve muscle growth and recovery all in one shake. The taste is magnificent and the results are even better when you need to train hard and want to see results.

Preparation:

Mix all the ingredients together in a juicer or blender at high speed and then enjoy a delicious shake.

Ingredients:

- ½ cup strawberries
- ¼ cup mixed berries (raspberries, blueberries and blackberries)
- ¼ cup organic pomegranate juice
- ¼ cup organic grape juice
- handful sliced almonds for topping
- 1 scoop Whey Protein Powder

Nutritional Facts:

- Calories:200
- Proteins: 31g
- Carbs: 19g
- Fat: 1g

OTHER GREAT TITLES BY THIS AUTHOR

Advanced Mental Toughness Training for Bodybuilders

Using Visualization to Push Yourself to the Limit

By

Joseph Correa

Certified Sports Nutritionist

Becoming Mentally Tougher in Bodybuilding by Using Meditation

Reach Your Potential by Controlling Your Inner Thoughts

By

Joseph Correa

Certified Sports Nutritionist

www.ingramcontent.com/pod-product-compliance
Lightning Source LLC
Chambersburg PA
CBHW071744080526
44588CB00013B/2142